JUST A CLOSER WALK

90 Day Breath Prayer Journal

DIANA LEAGH MATTHEWS

Just a Closer Walk: Breath Prayers for the
©2021 by Diana Leagh Matthews

ISBN-13: 978-1-7369727-0-0

Published by LynneLee Lane Publishing

Scripture quotations marked ESV are from The
Holy Bible, English Standard Version. ESV®
Text Edition: 2016. Copyright © 2001 by
Crossway Bibles, a publishing ministry of Good
News Publishers.

Dedicated to:

God almighty and to my Lord
and Savior, Jesus Christ

To the Reader

While writing *Just a Closer Walk: 90 Breath Prayers for Healthcare Professionals* my assistant, Theresa, suggested a companion breath prayer journal.

Although there is room for notes in the breath prayer books, we decided to provide more room for the reader to pour their heart out.

Whether you decide to use it as a companion piece to the breath prayer books or as a journal the book is intended to be a tool to express what is on your heart and explore each day's emotions.

There are 90 days to journal. In addition, there is also room to write prayers, Gratitude, and prayer request. There is also a place for song of the day to record one which touched your heart or ministered to you for the day. To go deeper there is room to go more in-depth with two additional sections.

The love in action provides space to write out ways you have exhibited love, compassion, and friendship to others.

The recharge and relax are to practice self-care and take care of oneself.

If you're anything like me, sometimes we just need room to hold ourselves accountable.

Ideally, it would be wonderful if we could all stretch ourselves and not duplicate any of these areas. Some of the sections may be easier to refrain from duplicating than others, but it is an achievable goal.

As you write, may you feel the peace of the Lord, through whatever may be on life's pathway.

To God be the glory.

Write on! Live on! Love on!

Leagh

Table of Contents

THIS JOURNAL IS THE PROPERTY OF

_____

DAY 1

♡

"He heals the brokenhearted and binds up their wounds."
Psalm 147:3

Lord,

_____

_____

_____

_____

_____

_____

_____

90 Day Prayer Journal

_____

_____

_____

_____

_____

_____

_____

_____

PRAYER NEEDS

1. _____

2. _____

3. _____

Love in Action

Song of the Day:

_____

GRATITUDE OF THE DAY:

1. _____

2. _____

3. _____

Recharge & Relax

*"As long as you live keep learning
how to live."*
Seneca

90 Day Prayer Journal

DAY 2

"The Lord your God is in your midst, a mighty one who will save; he will rejoice over you with gladness; he will quiet you by his love; he will exult over you with loud singing."
Zephaniah 3:17

Lord,

_____

_____

_____

_____

_____

_____

_____

_____

_____

_____

_____

_____

_____

PRAYER NEEDS

1. _____

2. _____

3._____

Love in Action

Song of the Day:

_____

GRATITUDE OF THE DAY:

1. _____

2. _____

3. _____

Recharge & Relax

"The servants of the Lord are to sing His praises in this life to the world's end; and in the next life world without end."
John Boys

DAY 3

"Know this, my beloved brothers: let every person be quick to hear, slow to speak, slow to anger."
James 1:19

Lord,

_____

_____

_____

_____

_____

_____

_____

_____

_____

_____

_____

_____

_____

_____

_____

PRAYER NEEDS

1. _____

2. _____

3. _____

Love in Action

Song of the Day:

_____

GRATITUDE OF THE DAY:

1. _____

2. _____

3. _____

Recharge & Relax

"As long as you live keep learning how to live."
Seneca

DAY 4

♡

"Above all, keep loving one another earnestly, since love covers a multitude of sins."
1 Peter 4:8

Lord,

_____

_____

_____

_____

_____

_____

90 Day Prayer Journal

_____

_____

_____

_____

_____

_____

_____

_____

_____

PRAYER NEEDS

1. _____

2. _____

3. _____

Love in Action

Song of the Day:

_____

GRATITUDE OF THE DAY:

1. _____

2. _____

3. _____

Recharge & Relax

"Wicked men obey from fear; good men, from love."
St. Augustine

DAY 5

"*Rejoice in hope, be patient in tribulation, be constant in prayer.*"
Romans 12:12

Lord,

_____

_____

_____

_____

_____

_____

_____

_____

_____

_____

_____

_____

_____

_____

_____

_____

PRAYER NEEDS

1. _____

2. _____

3. _____

Love in Action

Song of the Day:

_____

GRATITUDE OF THE DAY:

1. _____

2. _____

3. _____

Recharge & Relax

"Life is as tedious as a twice-told tale."
William Shakespeare

DAY 6

♡

"Casting all your anxieties on him,
because he cares for you."
1 Peter 5:7

Lord,

_____

_____

_____

_____

_____

_____

_____

90 Day Prayer Journal

_____

_____

_____

_____

_____

_____

_____

_____

PRAYER NEEDS

1. _____

2. _____

3._____

Love in Action

Song of the Day:

_____

GRATITUDE OF THE DAY:

1. _____

2. _____

3. _____

Recharge & Relax

"Worry is carrying a burden God never intended us to bear."
Unknown

DAY 7

"*It is better to live in a corner of the housetop than in a house shared with a quarrelsome wife.*"
Proverbs 21:9

Lord,

_____

_____

_____

_____

_____

_____

_____

_____

_____

_____

_____

_____

_____

_____

PRAYER NEEDS

1. _____

2. _____

3._____

Love in Action

Song of the Day:

_____

GRATITUDE OF THE DAY:

1. _____

2. _____

3._____

Recharge & Relax

*"The miserable have no other medicine
but only hope…"*
Fredrich Nietzsche

DAY 8

"*The Lord is good, a stronghold in the day of trouble; he knows those who take refuge in him.*"
Nahum 1:7

Lord,

_____

_____

_____

_____

_____

_____

90 Day Prayer Journal

_____

_____

_____

_____

_____

_____

_____

_____

_____

PRAYER NEEDS

1. _____

2. _____

3._____

Love in Action

Song of the Day:

_____

GRATITUDE OF THE DAY:

1. _____

2. _____

3. _____

Recharge & Relax

"Our walk counts far more than our talk, always!"
George Muller

DAY 9

"Do not be deceived: "Bad company ruins good morals."
1 Corinthians 15:33

Lord,

_____

_____

_____

_____

_____

_____

_____

_____

_____

_____

_____

_____

_____

_____

_____

_____

PRAYER NEEDS

1. _____

2. _____

3. _____

Love in Action

Song of the Day:

_____

GRATITUDE OF THE DAY:

1. _____

2. _____

3. _____

Recharge & Relax

*"The mind is not a vessel to be filled but
a fire to be kindled."*
Plutarch

DAY 10

"Let us not love in word or talk but in deed and in truth."
1 John 3:18

Lord,

_____

_____

_____

_____

_____

_____

_____

_____

_____

_____

_____

_____

_____

_____

_____

PRAYER NEEDS

1. _____

2. _____

3._____

Love in Action

Song of the Day:

_____

GRATITUDE OF THE DAY:

1. _____

2. _____

3. _____

Recharge & Relax

*"The single desire that dominated my
search for delight was simply to love
and to be loved."*
St. Augustine

DAY 11

"Do nothing from selfish ambition or conceit, but in humility count others more significant than yourselves."
Philippians 2:3

Lord,

_____

_____

_____

_____

_____

_____

_____

_____

_____

_____

_____

_____

_____

_____

PRAYER NEEDS

1. _____

2. _____

3._____

Love in Action

Song of the Day:

_____

GRATITUDE OF THE DAY:

1. _____

2. _____

3. _____

Recharge & Relax

"If you wish to win a man over to your ideas, first make him your friend."
Abraham Lincoln

DAY 12

"I lift up my eyes to the hills. From where does my help come? My help comes from the Lord, who made heaven and earth."
Psalm 121:1-2

Lord,

_____

_____

_____

_____

_____

_____

_____

_____

_____

_____

_____

_____

_____

_____

PRAYER NEEDS

1. _____

2. _____

3._____

Love in Action

Song of the Day:

_____

GRATITUDE OF THE DAY:

1. _____

2. _____

3. _____

> ### Recharge & Relax

"God sees us in secret; therefore, let us seek His face in secret. Though heaven be God's palace, yet it is not his prison."
Thomas Brooks

DAY 13

♡

"He made the storm be still, and the waves of the sea were hushed. Then they were glad that the waters were quiet, and he brought them to their desired haven."
Psalm 107:29-30

Lord,

_____

_____

_____

_____

_____

_____

90 Day Prayer Journal

_____

_____

_____

_____

_____

_____

_____

PRAYER NEEDS

1. _____

2. _____

3._____

Love in Action

Song of the Day:

_____

GRATITUDE OF THE DAY:

1. _____

2. _____

3._____

Recharge & Relax

*"He who has conquered doubt and fear
has conquered failure."*
James Lane Allen

DAY 14

"Come to me, all who labor and are heavy laden, and I will give you rest."
Matthew 11:28

Lord,

_____

_____

_____

_____

_____

_____

_____

_____

_____

_____

_____

_____

_____

_____

_____

PRAYER NEEDS

1. _____

2. _____

3._____

Love in Action

Song of the Day:

_____

GRATITUDE OF THE DAY:

1. _____

2. _____

3._____

Recharge & Relax

"God cannot give us a happiness and peace apart from Himself, because it is not there. There is no such thing."
C.S. Lewis

DAY 15

"*God is our refuge and strength, a very present help in trouble.*"
Psalm 46:1

Lord,

_____

_____

_____

_____

_____

_____

_____

90 Day Prayer Journal

_____

_____

_____

_____

_____

_____

_____

_____

PRAYER NEEDS

1. _____

2. _____

3. _____

Love in Action

Song of the Day:

_____

GRATITUDE OF THE DAY:

1. _____

2. _____

3. _____

> ### Recharge & Relax

*"The beginning is the most important
part of the work."*
Plato

DAY 16

"But Jesus looked at them and said,
'With man this is impossible, but with
God all things are possible.'"
Matthew 19:26

Lord,

_____

_____

_____

_____

_____

_____

_____

_____

_____

_____

_____

_____

_____

_____

PRAYER NEEDS

1. _____

2. _____

3. _____

Love in Action

Song of the Day:

_____

GRATITUDE OF THE DAY:

1. _____
2. _____
3._____

Recharge & Relax

"God loves with a great love the man whose heart is bursting with a passion for the impossible."
William Booth

DAY 17

"For God so loved the world, that he gave his only Son, that whoever believes in him should not perish but have eternal life."
John 3:16

Lord,

_____

_____

_____

_____

_____

_____

_____

_____

_____

_____

_____

_____

_____

_____

PRAYER NEEDS

1. _____

2. _____

3. _____

Love in Action

Song of the Day:

_____

GRATITUDE OF THE DAY:

1. _____

2. _____

3._____

Recharge & Relax

"There is no remedy for love but to love more."
Henry David Thoreau

DAY 18

"Better is a poor man who walks in his integrity than a rich man who is crooked in his ways."
Proverbs 28:6

Lord,

_____

_____

_____

_____

_____

_____

_____

90 Day Prayer Journal

_____

_____

_____

_____

_____

_____

_____

_____

～

PRAYER NEEDS

1. _____

2. _____

3. _____

Love in Action

Song of the Day:

_____

GRATITUDE OF THE DAY:

1. _____

2. _____

3. _____

Recharge & Relax

"Integrity is like the weather: Everybody talks about it but nobody knows what to do about it."
Stephen Carter

DAY 19

"Be kind to one another, tenderhearted, forgiving one another, as God in Christ forgave you."
Ephesians 4:32

Lord,

_____

_____

_____

_____

_____

_____

_____

_____

_____

_____

_____

_____

_____

_____

PRAYER NEEDS

1. _____

2. _____

3._____

Love in Action

Song of the Day:

_____

GRATITUDE OF THE DAY:

1. _____

2. _____

3._____

Recharge & Relax

*"Kindness is a language which the deaf
can hear and the blind can see."*
Mark Twain

DAY 20

♡

"A good man leaves an inheritance to his children's children, but the sinner's wealth is laid up for the righteous."
Proverbs 13:22

Lord,

_____

_____

_____

_____

_____

_____

_____

90 Day Prayer Journal

_____

_____

_____

_____

_____

_____

_____

PRAYER NEEDS

1. _____

2. _____

3. _____

Love in Action

Song of the Day:

_____

GRATITUDE OF THE DAY:

1. _____

2. _____

3. _____

Recharge & Relax

*"You can always give without loving,
but you can never love without giving."*
Amy Carmichael

DAY 21

"Let your speech always be gracious,
seasoned with salt, so that you may
know how you ought to answer
each person."
Colossians 4:6

Lord,

_____

_____

_____

_____

_____

_____

_____

_____

_____

_____

_____

_____

_____

_____

PRAYER NEEDS

1. _____

2. _____

3._____

Love in Action

Song of the Day:

_____

GRATITUDE OF THE DAY:

1. _____

2. _____

3. _____

Recharge & Relax

"It is one thing to be clever and another to be wise…"
George R. R. Martin

DAY 22

"I waited patiently for the Lord; he
inclined to me and heard my cry."
Psalm 40:1

Lord,

_____

_____

_____

_____

_____

_____

_____

_____

_____

_____

_____

_____

_____

_____

PRAYER NEEDS

1. _____

2. _____

3._____

Love in Action

Song of the Day:

_____

GRATITUDE OF THE DAY:

1. _____

2. _____

3._____

Recharge & Relax

"Patience is the grace of the man who could revenge himself, but chooses not to."
John Chrysostom

DAY 23

"He leads me in the paths of righteousness For His name's sake."
Psalm 23:3

Lord,

_____

_____

_____

_____

_____

_____

_____

_____

_____

_____

_____

_____

_____

_____

PRAYER NEEDS

1. _____

2. _____

3._____

Love in Action

Song of the Day:

_____

GRATITUDE OF THE DAY:

1. _____

2. _____

3._____

Recharge & Relax

*"For every minute you remain angry,
you give up sixty seconds of
peace of mind."*
Ralph Waldo Emerson

DAY 24

"A joyful heart is good medicine, but a crushed spirit dries up the bones."
Proverbs 17:22

Lord,

_____

_____

_____

_____

_____

_____

_____

_____

_____

_____

_____

_____

_____

_____

_____

PRAYER NEEDS

1. _____

2. _____

3._____

Love in Action

Song of the Day:

_____

GRATITUDE OF THE DAY:

1. _____

2. _____

3. _____

Recharge & Relax

"How sweet all at once it was for me to be rid of those fruitless joys which I had once feared to lose!…You drove them from me and took their place, you who are sweeter than all pleasure."
St. Augustine

DAY 25

"By wisdom a house is built, and by understanding it is established; by knowledge the rooms are filled with all precious and pleasant riches."
Proverbs 24:3-4

Lord,

_____

_____

_____

_____

_____

_____

_____

_____

_____

_____

_____

_____

_____

_____

_____

PRAYER NEEDS

1. _____

2. _____

3._____

Love in Action

Song of the Day:

_____

GRATITUDE OF THE DAY:

1. _____

2. _____

3. _____

Recharge & Relax

"A loving heart is the truest wisdom."
Charles Dickens

DAY 26

"Whoever brings blessing will be enriched, and one who waters will himself be watered."
Proverbs 11:25

Lord,

_____

_____

_____

_____

_____

_____

_____

_____

_____

_____

_____

_____

_____

_____

PRAYER NEEDS

1. _____

2. _____

3. _____

Love in Action

Song of the Day:

_____

GRATITUDE OF THE DAY:

1. _____

2. _____

3._____

Recharge & Relax

*"Faith brings a man empty to God,
that he may be filled with the
blessings of God."*
John Calvin

DAY 27

♡

"Bless those who curse you, pray for those who abuse you."
Luke 6:28

Lord,

_____

_____

_____

_____

_____

_____

_____

_____

_____

_____

_____

_____

_____

_____

_____

PRAYER NEEDS

1. _____

2. _____

3. _____

Love in Action

Song of the Day:

_____

GRATITUDE OF THE DAY:

1. _____

2. _____

3. _____

Recharge & Relax

"The value of an idea lies in the using of it."
Thomas A. Edison

DAY 28

"My flesh and my heart may fail, but God is the strength of my heart and my portion forever."
Psalm 73:26

Lord,

_____

_____

_____

_____

_____

_____

_____

_____

_____

_____

_____

_____

_____

_____

PRAYER NEEDS

1. _____

2. _____

3. _____

Love in Action

Song of the Day:

_____

GRATITUDE OF THE DAY:

1. _____

2. _____

3._____

Recharge & Relax

"The strength and happiness of a man consists in finding out the way in which God is going, and going that way too."
Henry Ward Beecher

DAY 29

"The God who equipped me with strength and made my way blameless."
Psalm 18:32

Lord,

_____

_____

_____

_____

_____

_____

_____

90 Day Prayer Journal

_____

_____

_____

_____

_____

_____

_____

_____

~

PRAYER NEEDS

1. _____

2. _____

3. _____

Love in Action

Song of the Day:

_____

GRATITUDE OF THE DAY:

1. _____

2. _____

3._____

Recharge & Relax

"It is not what happens to you, but how you react to it that matters."
Epictetus

DAY 30

"And let us not grow weary of doing good, for in due season we will reap, if we do not give up."
Galatians 6:9

Lord,

_____

_____

_____

_____

_____

_____

_____

90 Day Prayer Journal

_____

_____

_____

_____

_____

_____

_____

~∞~

PRAYER NEEDS

1. _____

2. _____

3. _____

Love in Action

Song of the Day:

_____

GRATITUDE OF THE DAY:

1. _____

2. _____

3. _____

Recharge & Relax

"If it were possible for me to alter any part of his plan, I could only spoil it."
John Newton

DAY 31

"Do not be anxious about anything, but in everything by prayer and supplication with thanksgiving let your requests be made known to God."
Philippians 4:6

Lord,

_____

_____

_____

_____

_____

_____

_____

_____

_____

_____

_____

_____

_____

_____

PRAYER NEEDS

1. _____

2. _____

3. _____

Love in Action

Song of the Day:

_____

GRATITUDE OF THE DAY:

1. _____

2. _____

3. _____

Recharge & Relax

*"The good we do today becomes the
happiness of tomorrow."*
William James

DAY 32

♡

*"Ask, and it will be given to you; seek,
and you will find; knock, and it will be
opened to you."*
Matthew 7:7

Lord,

_____

_____

_____

_____

_____

_____

_____

_____

_____

_____

_____

_____

_____

PRAYER NEEDS

1. _____

2. _____

3. _____

Love in Action

Song of the Day:

_____

GRATITUDE OF THE DAY:

1. _____

2. _____

3. _____

Recharge & Relax

Understanding is the reward of faith.
Therefore seek not to understand that
you may believe, but believe that you
may understand.
St. Augustine

DAY 33

"Trust in the Lord with all your heart, and do not lean on your own understanding."
Proverbs 3:5

Lord,

_____

_____

_____

_____

_____

_____

_____

_____

_____

_____

_____

_____

_____

PRAYER NEEDS

1. _____

2. _____

3._____

Love in Action

Song of the Day:

_____

GRATITUDE OF THE DAY:

1. _____

2. _____

3._____

Recharge & Relax

"Time ripens all things; no man is born wise..."
Miguel De Cervantes

DAY 34

"*Whoever is slow to anger has great understanding, but he who has a hasty temper exalts folly.*"
Proverbs 14:29

Lord,

_____

_____

_____

_____

_____

_____

_____

_____

_____

_____

_____

_____

_____

PRAYER NEEDS

1. _____

2. _____

3._____

Love in Action

Song of the Day:

_____

GRATITUDE OF THE DAY:

1. _____

2. _____

3. _____

Recharge & Relax

"It is a dangerous crisis when a proud heart meets with flattering lips."
John Flavel

DAY 35

*"And the King will answer them,
'Truly, I say to you, as you did it to one
of the least of these my brothers, you
did it to me.'"*
Matthew 25:40

Lord,

_____

_____

_____

_____

_____

_____

_____

_____

_____

_____

_____

_____

_____

_____

_____

PRAYER NEEDS

1. _____

2. _____

3._____

Love in Action

Song of the Day:

_____

GRATITUDE OF THE DAY:

1. _____

2. _____

3._____

Recharge & Relax

"Friendship is a single soul dwelling in two bodies."
Aristotle

DAY 36

"Count it all joy, my brothers, when you meet trials of various kinds, for you know that the testing of your faith produces steadfastness."
James 1:2-3

Lord,

_____

_____

_____

_____

_____

_____

_____

_____

_____

_____

_____

_____

_____

_____

PRAYER NEEDS

1. _____

2. _____

3._____

Love in Action

Song of the Day:

_____

GRATITUDE OF THE DAY:

1. _____

2. _____

3. _____

Recharge & Relax

*"The first and the great work of a
Christian is about his heart."*
Jonathan Edwards

DAY 37

"I was pushed hard, so that I was falling, but the Lord helped me."
Psalm 118:13

Lord,

_____

_____

_____

_____

_____

_____

90 Day Prayer Journal

_____

_____

_____

_____

_____

_____

_____

_____

PRAYER NEEDS

1. _____

2. _____

3._____

Love in Action

Song of the Day:

_____

GRATITUDE OF THE DAY:

1. _____

2. _____

3._____

Recharge & Relax

"Be yourself; everyone else is already taken."
Oscar Wilde

DAY 38

"Cast your burden on the Lord, and he will sustain you; he will never permit the righteous to be moved."
Psalm 55:22

Lord,

_____

_____

_____

_____

_____

_____

_____

_____

_____

_____

_____

_____

_____

_____

PRAYER NEEDS

1. _____

2. _____

3. _____

Love in Action

Song of the Day:

_____

GRATITUDE OF THE DAY:

1. _____

2. _____

3. _____

Recharge & Relax

"Every tomorrow has two handles. We can take hold of it with the handle of anxiety or the handle of faith."
Henry Ward Beecher

DAY 39

*"Bear one another's burdens, and so
fulfill the law of Christ."*
Galatians 6:2

Lord,

_____

_____

_____

_____

_____

_____

_____

_____

_____

_____

_____

_____

_____

_____

_____

PRAYER NEEDS

1. _____

2. _____

3._____

Love in Action

Song of the Day:

_____

GRATITUDE OF THE DAY:

1. _____

2. _____

3._____

Recharge & Relax

*"I destroy my enemies when I make
them my friends."*
Abraham Lincoln

DAY 40

"*A soft answer turns away wrath, but a harsh word stirs up anger.*"
Proverbs 15:1

Lord,

_____

_____

_____

_____

_____

_____

_____

_____

_____

_____

_____

_____

_____

_____

PRAYER NEEDS

1. _____

2. _____

3._____

Love in Action

Song of the Day:

_____

GRATITUDE OF THE DAY:

1. _____

2. _____

3._____

Recharge & Relax

"No matter how just your words may be, you ruin everything when you speak with anger."
John Chrysostom

DAY 41

"Keep your heart with all vigilance, for from it flow the springs of life."
Proverbs 4:23

Lord,

_____

_____

_____

_____

_____

_____

_____

_____

_____

_____

_____

_____

_____

_____

_____

90 Day Prayer Journal

PRAYER NEEDS

1. _____

2. _____

3._____

Love in Action

Song of the Day:

_____

GRATITUDE OF THE DAY:

1. _____

2. _____

3._____

Recharge & Relax

"It is better to be alone than in bad company."
George Washington

DAY 42

♡

"Rejoice always, pray without ceasing, give thanks in all circumstances; for this is the will of God in Christ Jesus for you."
1 Thessalonians 5:16-18

Lord,

_____

_____

_____

_____

_____

_____

_____

_____

_____

_____

_____

_____

_____

_____

PRAYER NEEDS

1. _____

2. _____

3. _____

Love in Action

Song of the Day:

_____

GRATITUDE OF THE DAY:

1. _____

2. _____

3._____

Recharge & Relax

"When a man no longer seeks his comfort from any creature, then he first begins to enjoy God perfectly, and he will be well content with whatever befalls him."
Thomas A. Kempis

DAY 43

"Love is patient and kind; love does not envy or boast; it is not arrogant."
1 Corinthians 13:4

Lord,

_____

_____

_____

_____

_____

_____

_____

_____

_____

_____

_____

_____

_____

_____

_____

_____

PRAYER NEEDS

1. _____

2. _____

3._____

Love in Action

Song of the Day:

_____

GRATITUDE OF THE DAY:

1. _____

2. _____

3._____

Recharge & Relax

*"Love inspires, illuminates, designates,
and leads the way."*
Mary Baker Eddy

DAY 44

♡

"Consider the ravens: they neither sow nor reap, they have neither storehouse nor barn, and yet God feeds them. Of how much more value are you than the birds!"
Luke 12:24

Lord,

_____

_____

_____

_____

_____

_____

_____

_____

_____

_____

_____

_____

_____

PRAYER NEEDS

1. _____

2. _____

3. _____

Love in Action

Song of the Day:

_____

GRATITUDE OF THE DAY:

1. _____

2. _____

3. _____

Recharge & Relax

"Then he will neither rejoice over having much, nor grieve over having little, but will commit himself fully and trustfully to God, who is all in all to him."
Thomas A. Kempis

DAY 45

"Peace I leave with you; my peace I give to you. Not as the world gives do I give to you. Let not your hearts be troubled, neither let them be afraid."
John 14:27

Lord,

_____

_____

_____

_____

_____

_____

PRAYER NEEDS

1. _____

2. _____

3._____

Love in Action

Song of the Day:

_____

GRATITUDE OF THE DAY:

1. _____

2. _____

3. _____

Recharge & Relax

"I am not afraid; I was born to do this."
Joan of Arc

DAY 46

"Be strong and courageous. Do not fear or be in dread of them, for it is the Lord your God who goes with you. He will not leave you or forsake you."
Deuteronomy 31:6

Lord,

_____

_____

_____

_____

_____

_____

_____

_____

_____

_____

_____

_____

_____

_____

PRAYER NEEDS

1. _____

2. _____

3._____

Love in Action

Song of the Day:

_____

GRATITUDE OF THE DAY:

1. _____

2. _____

3. _____

Recharge & Relax

"As you obey God's Word and rely on His strengthening power, you can count on biblical change to occur in every area of your life."
John Broger

DAY 47

"Rejoice always, pray without ceasing, give thanks in all circumstances; for this is the will of God in Christ Jesus for you."
1 Thessalonians 5:16-18

Lord,

_____

_____

_____

_____

_____

_____

90 Day Prayer Journal

_____

_____

_____

_____

_____

_____

_____

_____

_____

PRAYER NEEDS

1. _____

2. _____

3. _____

Love in Action

Song of the Day:

_____

GRATITUDE OF THE DAY:

1. _____

2. _____

3._____

Recharge & Relax

*"Without music, life would
be a mistake."*
Friedrich Nietzsche

DAY 48

♡

"Wait for the Lord; be strong, and let
your heart take courage;
wait for the Lord!"
Psalms 27:14

Lord,

_____

_____

_____

_____

_____

_____

_____

_____

_____

_____

_____

_____

_____

_____

PRAYER NEEDS

1. _____

2. _____

3._____

Love in Action

Song of the Day:

_____

GRATITUDE OF THE DAY:

1. _____

2. _____

3._____

Recharge & Relax

"When led of the Spirit, the child of God must be as ready to wait as to go, as prepared to be silent as to speak."
Lewis Sperry Chafer

DAY 49

"*Do not neglect to show hospitality to strangers, for thereby some have entertained angels unawares.*"
Hebrews 13:2

Lord,

_____

_____

_____

_____

_____

_____

_____

_____

_____

_____

_____

_____

_____

_____

PRAYER NEEDS

1. _____

2. _____

3._____

Love in Action

Song of the Day:

_____

GRATITUDE OF THE DAY:

1. _____

2. _____

3. _____

Recharge & Relax

"A superior man is modest in his speech, but exceeds in his actions."
Confucius

DAY 50

"I believe that I shall look upon the goodness of the Lord in the land of the living! Wait for the Lord; be strong, and let your heart take courage; wait for the Lord!"
Psalm 27:13-14

Lord,

_____

_____

_____

_____

_____

_____

_____

_____

_____

_____

_____

_____

_____

_____

PRAYER NEEDS

1. _____

2. _____

3. _____

Love in Action

Song of the Day:

_____

GRATITUDE OF THE DAY:

1. _____

2. _____

3. _____

Recharge & Relax

*"To wait is not to sit with folded hands,
but to learn to do what we are told."*
Oswald Chambers

DAY 51

"He will wipe away every tear from their eyes, and death shall be no more, neither shall there be mourning, nor crying, nor pain anymore, for the former things have passed away."
Revelation 21:4

Lord,

_____

_____

_____

_____

_____

_____

_____

_____

_____

_____

_____

_____

_____

_____

PRAYER NEEDS

1. _____

2. _____

3._____

Love in Action

Song of the Day:

_____

GRATITUDE OF THE DAY:

1. _____

2. _____

3._____

Recharge & Relax

"For every minutes you are angry you lose sixty seconds of happiness."
Ralph Waldo Emerson

DAY 52

"With all humility and gentleness, with patience, bearing with one another in love."
Ephesians 4:2

Lord,

_____

_____

_____

_____

_____

_____

_____

_____

_____

_____

_____

_____

_____

_____

PRAYER NEEDS

1. _____

2. _____

3._____

Love in Action

Song of the Day:

_____

GRATITUDE OF THE DAY:

1. _____

2. _____

3. _____

Recharge & Relax

"Trust the past to God's mercy, the present to God's love and the future to God's providence."
St. Augustine

DAY 53

♡

*"Do you not know that you are God's
temple and that God's Spirit
dwells in you?"*
1 Corinthians 3:16

Lord,

_____

_____

_____

_____

_____

_____

_____

_____

_____

_____

_____

_____

_____

PRAYER NEEDS

1. _____

2. _____

3. _____

Love in Action

Song of the Day:

_____

GRATITUDE OF THE DAY:

1. _____

2. _____

3. _____

> ### Recharge & Relax

"Reading is to the mind what exercise is to the body."
Joseph Addison

DAY 54

"And my God will supply every need of yours according to his riches in glory in Christ Jesus."
Philippians 4:19

Lord,

_____

_____

_____

_____

_____

_____

90 Day Prayer Journal

_____

_____

_____

_____

_____

_____

_____

PRAYER NEEDS

1. _____

2. _____

3._____

Love in Action

Song of the Day:

_____

GRATITUDE OF THE DAY:

1. _____

2. _____

3. _____

Recharge & Relax

"The Spirit never loosens where the Word binds; the Spirit never justifies where the Word condemns; the Spirit never approves where the Word disapproves; the Spirit never blesses where the Word curses."
Thomas Brooks

DAY 55

"And we know that for those who love God all things work together for good, for those who are called according to his purpose."
Romans 8:28

Lord,

_____

_____

_____

_____

_____

_____

_____

_____

_____

_____

_____

_____

_____

_____

PRAYER NEEDS

1. _____

2. _____

3._____

Love in Action

Song of the Day:

_____

GRATITUDE OF THE DAY:

1. _____

2. _____

3._____

Recharge & Relax

*"To love another person is to see the
face of God."*
Victor Hugo

DAY 56

♡

"As each has received a gift, use it to serve one another, as good stewards of God's varied grace."
1 Peter 4:10

Lord,

_____

_____

_____

_____

_____

_____

_____

_____

_____

_____

_____

_____

_____

_____

PRAYER NEEDS

1. _____

2. _____

3. _____

Love in Action

Song of the Day:

_____

GRATITUDE OF THE DAY:

1. _____

2. _____

3. _____

Recharge & Relax

"There are two things to do about the gospel: believe it and behave it."
Susanna Wesley

DAY 57

"And those who know your name put
their trust in you, for you, O Lord, have
not forsaken those who seek you."
Psalm 9:10

Lord,

_____

_____

_____

_____

_____

_____

90 Day Prayer Journal

_____

_____

_____

_____

_____

_____

_____

_____

PRAYER NEEDS

1. _____

2. _____

3._____

Love in Action

Song of the Day:

_____

GRATITUDE OF THE DAY:

1. _____

2. _____

3. _____

Recharge & Relax

*"The noblest pleasure is the
joy of understanding."*
Leonardo da Vinci

DAY 58

♡

"Have you not known? Have you not heard? The Lord is the everlasting God, the Creator of the ends of the earth. He does not faint or grow weary; his understanding is unsearchable."
Isaiah 40:28

Lord,

_____

_____

_____

_____

_____

_____

90 Day Prayer Journal

_____

_____

_____

_____

_____

_____

_____

～

PRAYER NEEDS

1. _____

2. _____

3. _____

Love in Action

Song of the Day:

_____

GRATITUDE OF THE DAY:

1. _____

2. _____

3._____

Recharge & Relax

"If you have no joy, there's a leak in your Christianity somewhere."
Billy Sunday

DAY 59

"*But they who wait for the Lord shall renew their strength; they shall mount up with wings like eagles; they shall run and not be weary; they shall walk and not faint.*"
Isaiah 40:31

Lord,

_____

_____

_____

_____

_____

_____

90 Day Prayer Journal

_____

_____

_____

_____

_____

_____

_____

245

PRAYER NEEDS

1. _____

2. _____

3._____

Love in Action

Song of the Day:

_____

GRATITUDE OF THE DAY:

1. _____

2. _____

3. _____

Recharge & Relax

*"Compromise makes a good umbrella
but a poor roof."*
James Russell Lowell

DAY 60

"*For where your treasure is, there your heart will be also.*"
Matthew 6:21

Lord,

_____

_____

_____

_____

_____

_____

_____

_____

_____

_____

_____

_____

_____

_____

_____

_____

PRAYER NEEDS

1. _____

2. _____

3. _____

Love in Action

Song of the Day:

_____

GRATITUDE OF THE DAY:

1. _____

2. _____

3. _____

Recharge & Relax

"Where your pleasure is, there is your treasure; Where your treasure is, there is your heart; Where your heart is, there is your happiness."
St. Augustine

DAY 61

"The young lions suffer want and hunger; but those who seek the Lord lack no good thing."
Psalm 34:10

Lord,

_____

_____

_____

_____

_____

_____

_____

_____

_____

_____

_____

_____

_____

_____

PRAYER NEEDS

1. _____

2. _____

3._____

Love in Action

Song of the Day:

GRATITUDE OF THE DAY:

1. _____

2. _____

3._____

Recharge & Relax

"The most useless are those who never change through the years."
James M. Barrie

DAY 62

"Great is our Lord, and abundant in power; his understanding is beyond measure."
Psalm 147:5

Lord,

_____

_____

_____

_____

_____

_____

_____

_____

_____

_____

_____

_____

_____

_____

_____

PRAYER NEEDS

1. _____

2. _____

3._____

Love in Action

Song of the Day:

_____

GRATITUDE OF THE DAY:

1. _____

2. _____

3._____

Recharge & Relax

*"Wherever he has a tent, God should
have an altar."*
James Alexander

DAY 63

"For everything there is a season, and a time for every matter under heaven."
Ecclesiastes 3:1

Lord,

_____

_____

_____

_____

_____

_____

_____

_____

_____

_____

_____

_____

_____

_____

PRAYER NEEDS

1. _____

2. _____

3._____

Love in Action

Song of the Day:

_____

GRATITUDE OF THE DAY:

1. _____

2. _____

3._____

Recharge & Relax

"Life is a balance of holding on and letting go."
Rumi

DAY 64

♡

"And God is able to make all grace abound to you, so that having all sufficiency in all things at all times, you may abound in every good work."
2 Corinthians 9:8

Lord,

_____

_____

_____

_____

_____

_____

90 Day Prayer Journal

_____

_____

_____

_____

_____

_____

_____

_____

_____

PRAYER NEEDS

1. _____

2. _____

3._____

Love in Action

Song of the Day:

_____

GRATITUDE OF THE DAY:

1. _____

2. _____

3._____

Recharge & Relax

*"The servants of the Lord are to sing
His praises in this life to the world's
end; and in the next life
world without end."*
John Boys

DAY 65

"God is our refuge and strength, a very present help in trouble."
Psalm 46:1

Lord,

_____

_____

_____

_____

_____

_____

_____

_____

_____

PRAYER NEEDS

1. _____

2. _____

3._____

> ### *Love in Action*

Song of the Day:

_____

GRATITUDE OF THE DAY:

1. _____

2. _____

3._____

Recharge & Relax

*"A person often meets his destiny on the
road he took to avoid it."*
Jean de la Fontaine

DAY 66

"So as to walk in a manner worthy of the Lord, fully pleasing to him: bearing fruit in every good work and increasing in the knowledge of God."
Colossians 1:10

Lord,

_____

_____

_____

_____

_____

_____

90 Day Prayer Journal

_____

_____

_____

_____

_____

_____

_____

_____

PRAYER NEEDS

1. _____

2. _____

3._____

Love in Action

Song of the Day:

_____

GRATITUDE OF THE DAY:

1. _____

2. _____

3. _____

Recharge & Relax

"Those who fall away have never been thoroughly imbued with the knowledge of Christ but only had a slight and passing taste of it."
John Calvin

DAY 67

"And as you wish that others would do to you, do so to them."
Luke 6:31

Lord,

_____

_____

_____

_____

_____

_____

_____

_____

_____

_____

_____

_____

_____

_____

PRAYER NEEDS

1. _____

2. _____

3._____

Love in Action

Song of the Day:

_____

GRATITUDE OF THE DAY:

1. _____

2. _____

3. _____

Recharge & Relax

"Wise men speak because they have something to say; fools because they have to say something."
Plato

DAY 68

"He heals the brokenhearted and binds up their wounds."
Psalm 147:3

Lord,

_____

_____

_____

_____

_____

_____

_____

90 Day Prayer Journal

_____

_____

_____

_____

_____

_____

_____

_____

PRAYER NEEDS

1. _____

2. _____

3._____

Love in Action

Song of the Day:

_____

GRATITUDE OF THE DAY:

1. _____

2. _____

3. _____

Recharge & Relax

"Christ's wounds are thy healings, His agonies thy repose, His conflicts thy conquests, His groans thy songs, His pains thine ease, His shame thy glory, His death thy life, His sufferings thy salvation."
Matthew Henry

DAY 69

"*Let each of you look not only to his own interests, but also to the interests of others.*"
Philippians 2:4

Lord,

_____

_____

_____

_____

_____

_____

_____

PRAYER NEEDS

1. _____

2. _____

3._____

Love in Action

Song of the Day:

_____

GRATITUDE OF THE DAY:

1. _____

2. _____

3. _____

Recharge & Relax

"If your actions inspire others to dream more, learn more, do more and become more, you are a leader."
John Quincy Adams

DAY 70

"Then he said to his disciples, "The harvest is plentiful, but the laborers are few; therefore pray earnestly to the Lord of the harvest to send out laborers into his harvest."
Mathew 9:37-38

Lord,

_____

_____

_____

_____

_____

_____

_____

_____

_____

_____

_____

_____

_____

_____

PRAYER NEEDS

1. _____

2. _____

3._____

Love in Action

Song of the Day:

_____

GRATITUDE OF THE DAY:

1. _____

2. _____

3. _____

Recharge & Relax

"Many, I fear, would like glory, who have no wish for grace. They would [want to] have the wages, but not the work; the harvest, but not the labor; the reaping, but not the sowing; the reward, but not the battle. But it may not be."
J.C. Ryle

DAY 71

"Therefore, since we are surrounded by so great a cloud of witnesses, let us also lay aside every weight, and sin which clings so closely, and let us run with endurance the race that is set before us."
Hebrews 12:1

Lord,

_____

_____

_____

_____

_____

90 Day Prayer Journal

_____

_____

_____

_____

_____

_____

_____

_____

_____

90 Day Prayer Journal

~∽~

PRAYER NEEDS

1. _____

2. _____

3._____

Love in Action

Song of the Day:

_____

GRATITUDE OF THE DAY:

1. _____

2. _____

3._____

Recharge & Relax

*"Don't judge each day by the harvest
you reap but by the seeds
that you plant."*
Robert Louis Stevenson

DAY 72

"*For I know the plans I have for you,
declares the Lord, plans for welfare and
not for evil, to give you
a future and a hope.*"
Jeremiah 29:11

Lord,

_____

_____

_____

_____

_____

_____

_____

_____

_____

_____

_____

_____

_____

_____

PRAYER NEEDS

1. _____

2. _____

3._____

Love in Action

Song of the Day:

_____

GRATITUDE OF THE DAY:

1. _____

2. _____

3. _____

Recharge & Relax

"Don't dig up in doubt what you planted in faith."
Elisabeth Elliot

DAY 73

"*Behold, I am doing a new thing; now it springs forth, do you not perceive it? I will make a way in the wilderness and rivers in the desert.*"
Isaiah 43:19

Lord,

_____

_____

_____

_____

_____

_____

_____

_____

_____

_____

_____

_____

_____

_____

PRAYER NEEDS

1. _____

2. _____

3. _____

Love in Action

Song of the Day:

_____

🌷

GRATITUDE OF THE DAY:

1. _____

2. _____

3._____

Recharge & Relax

*"Experience is the teacher
of all things."
Julius Caesar*

DAY 74

"For you equipped me with strength for the battle; you made those who rise against me sink under me."
Psalm 18:39

Lord,

_____

_____

_____

_____

_____

_____

_____

_____

_____

_____

_____

_____

_____

_____

_____

~∞~

PRAYER NEEDS

1. _____

2. _____

3. _____

Love in Action

Song of the Day:

_____

GRATITUDE OF THE DAY:

1. _____

2. _____

3._____

Recharge & Relax

"We never find out the strength of the evil impulse inside us until we try to fight it."
C.S. Lewis

DAY 75

"For even the Son of Man came not to be served but to serve, and to give his life as a ransom for many."
Mark 10:45

Lord,

_____

_____

_____

_____

_____

_____

_____

_____

_____

_____

_____

_____

_____

_____

PRAYER NEEDS

1. _____

2. _____

3._____

Love in Action

Song of the Day:

_____

GRATITUDE OF THE DAY:

1. _____

2. _____

3. _____

Recharge & Relax

*"If you suffer thank God it is a sure
sign that you are alive."*
Elbert Hubbard

DAY 76

♡

"And let us not grow weary of doing good, for in due season we will reap, if we do not give up."
Galatians 6:9

Lord,

_____

_____

_____

_____

_____

_____

_____

_____

_____

_____

_____

_____

_____

PRAYER NEEDS

1. _____

2. _____

3._____

Love in Action

Song of the Day:

_____

GRATITUDE OF THE DAY:

1. _____

2. _____

3._____

> *Recharge & Relax*

"What can God have that gives Him greater satisfaction than that a thousand times a day all His creatures should thus pause to withdraw and worship him in the heart?"
Brother Lawrence

DAY 77

"So we do not lose heart. Though our outer self is wasting away, our inner self is being renewed day by day."
2 Corinthians 4:16

Lord,

_____

_____

_____

_____

_____

_____

_____

_____

_____

_____

_____

_____

_____

PRAYER NEEDS

1. _____

2. _____

3._____

Love in Action

Song of the Day:

_____

GRATITUDE OF THE DAY:

1. _____

2. _____

3. _____

Recharge & Relax

*"The greatest test of courage on earth is
to bear defeat without losing heart."*
Robert Green Ingersoll

DAY 78

"Therefore, my beloved brothers, be steadfast, immovable, always abounding in the work of the Lord, knowing that in the Lord your labor is not in vain."
1 Corinthians 15:58

Lord,

_____

_____

_____

_____

_____

_____

_____

_____

_____

_____

_____

_____

_____

_____

PRAYER NEEDS

1. _____

2. _____

3._____

Love in Action

Song of the Day:

_____

GRATITUDE OF THE DAY:

1. _____

2. _____

3._____

Recharge & Relax

"He did not redeem us by a little loss, a little sacrifice, a little labor, a little suffering. "He redeemed us to God by his blood," "the precious blood of Christ" (Rev 5:9; 1Pe 1:19). He gave all He had, even His life, for us."
Horatius Bonar

DAY 79

"Set your minds on things that are above, not on things that are on earth."
Colossians 3:2

Lord,

_____

_____

_____

_____

_____

_____

_____

PRAYER NEEDS

1. _____

2. _____

3._____

Love in Action

Song of the Day:

_____

GRATITUDE OF THE DAY:

1. _____

2. _____

3. _____

Recharge & Relax

"In all things of nature, there is something of the marvelous."
Aristotle

DAY 80

"The Lord is my strength and my song, and he has become my salvation; this is my God, and I will praise him, my father's God, and I will exalt him."
Exodus 15:2

Lord,

_____

_____

_____

_____

_____

_____

_____

_____

_____

_____

_____

_____

_____

PRAYER NEEDS

1. _____

2. _____

3. _____

Love in Action

Song of the Day:

_____

GRATITUDE OF THE DAY:

1. _____

2. _____

3. _____

Recharge & Relax

"There is no prayer acknowledged, approved, accepted, recorded, or rewarded by God, but that wherein the heart is sincerely and wholly."
Thomas Brooks

DAY 81

*"The Lord is near to the brokenhearted
and saves the crushed in spirit."*
Psalm 34:18

Lord,

_____

_____

_____

_____

_____

_____

_____

_____

_____

_____

_____

_____

_____

_____

_____

PRAYER NEEDS

1. _____

2. _____

3._____

Love in Action

Song of the Day:

_____

GRATITUDE OF THE DAY:

1. _____

2. _____

3. _____

Recharge & Relax

"We can complain because rose bushes have thorns, or rejoice because thorn bushes have roses."
Abraham Lincoln

DAY 82

"In the same way, let your light shine before others, so that they may see your good works and give glory to your Father who is in heaven."
Matthew 5:16

Lord,

_____

_____

_____

_____

_____

_____

_____

_____

_____

_____

_____

_____

_____

PRAYER NEEDS

1. _____

2. _____

3._____

Love in Action

Song of the Day:

_____

GRATITUDE OF THE DAY:

1. _____

2. _____

3. _____

Recharge & Relax

"God is glorified not only by His glory's being seen, but by its being rejoiced in."
Jonathan Edwards

DAY 83

"Do not neglect to do good and to share what you have, for such sacrifices are pleasing to God."
Hebrews 13:16

Lord,

_____

_____

_____

_____

_____

_____

_____

_____

_____

_____

_____

_____

_____

_____

PRAYER NEEDS

1. _____

2. _____

3._____

Love in Action

Song of the Day:

_____

GRATITUDE OF THE DAY:

1. _____

2. _____

3. _____

Recharge & Relax

"The things we love tell us
what we are."
St. Thomas Aquinas

DAY 84

♡

"I can do all things through him who strengthens me."
Philippians 4:13

Lord,

_____

_____

_____

_____

_____

_____

_____

90 Day Prayer Journal

_____

_____

_____

_____

_____

_____

_____

_____

~

PRAYER NEEDS

1. _____

2. _____

3. _____

Love in Action

Song of the Day:

_____

GRATITUDE OF THE DAY:

1. _____

2. _____

3._____

Recharge & Relax

"A proud man is always looking down on things and people: and, of course, as long as you are looking down, you cannot see something that is above you."
C.S. Lewis

DAY 85

"Now set your mind and heart to seek the LORD your God. "
1 Chronicles 22:19

Lord,

_____

_____

_____

_____

_____

_____

_____

_____

_____

_____

_____

_____

_____

_____

~

PRAYER NEEDS

1. _____

2. _____

3. _____

Love in Action

Song of the Day:

_____

GRATITUDE OF THE DAY:

1. _____

2. _____

3. _____

Recharge & Relax

"Sometimes the people with the worst past, create the best future."
Umar ibn Al-Khattab

DAY 86

"Be kind to one another, tenderhearted, forgiving one another, as God in Christ forgave you."
Ephesians 4:32

Lord,

_____

_____

_____

_____

_____

_____

_____

90 Day Prayer Journal

_____

_____

_____

_____

_____

_____

_____

PRAYER NEEDS

1. _____

2. _____

3. _____

Love in Action

Song of the Day:

_____

GRATITUDE OF THE DAY:

1. _____

2. _____

3. _____

Recharge & Relax

"The only way to learn strong faith is to endure great trials. I have learned my faith by standing firm amid severe testings."
George Muller

DAY 87

"Do not be conformed to this world, but be transformed by the renewal of your mind, that by testing you may discern what is the will of God, what is good and acceptable and perfect."
Romans 12:2

Lord,

_____

_____

_____

_____

_____

_____

_____

_____

_____

_____

_____

_____

_____

_____

PRAYER NEEDS

1. _____

2. _____

3._____

Love in Action

Song of the Day:

_____

GRATITUDE OF THE DAY:

1. _____

2. _____

3._____

Recharge & Relax

"You cannot escape the responsibility of tomorrow by evading it today."
Abraham Lincoln

DAY 88

The Lord is my light and my salvation; whom shall I fear? The Lord is the stronghold of my life; of whom shall I be afraid?"
Psalm 27:1

Lord,

_____

_____

_____

_____

_____

_____

90 Day Prayer Journal

_____

_____

_____

_____

_____

_____

_____

_____

_____

PRAYER NEEDS

1. _____

2. _____

3._____

Love in Action

Song of the Day:

_____

GRATITUDE OF THE DAY:

1. _____

2. _____

3._____

Recharge & Relax

*"In ourselves we are scattered, in Christ
we are gathered together."*
John Calvin

DAY 89

"But for you, O Lord, do I wait; it is you, O Lord my God, who will answer."
Psalm 38:15

Lord,

_____

_____

_____

_____

_____

_____

_____

_____

_____

_____

_____

_____

_____

_____

_____

_____

PRAYER NEEDS

1. _____

2. _____

3. _____

Love in Action

Song of the Day:

_____

GRATITUDE OF THE DAY:

1. _____

2. _____

3. _____

Recharge & Relax

*"Our greatest glory is not in never
failing, but in rising every time we fall."*
Confucius

DAY 90

*"Trust in the Lord with all your heart,
and do not lean on your own
understanding. In all your ways
acknowledge him, and he will make
straight your paths."
Proverbs 3:5-6*

Lord,

_____

_____

_____

_____

_____

_____

90 Day Prayer Journal

_____

_____

_____

_____

_____

_____

_____

PRAYER NEEDS

1. _____

2. _____

3. _____

Love in Action

Song of the Day:

_____

GRATITUDE OF THE DAY:

1. _____

2. _____

3._____

Recharge & Relax

*"Walk through every open door; be ready
in season and out of season as if
everything depended on your
labor...work as if everything depended on
your diligence, and trust in the blessing
of the Lord to bring success."*
George Muller

Diana Leagh Matthews is a writer, speaker, vocalist, Bible teacher, semi-professional genealogist and amateur historian.

She has worked in healthcare for seven years. For the last five years, she has served as an Activity director at a busy rehab and skilled nursing facility. She is a certified activity director and is finishing her certification as an activity consultant.

Her years in healthcare have given her a heart for others in the field and the stresses and issues faced on a daily basis.

She has also served as a caregiver and has a heart for caregivers and individuals living with dementia.

Leagh {pronounced as L-e-e-} has been published in numerous anthologies including the award-winning Moments with Billy Graham; Pandemic Moments; Wit, Whimsy, & Wisdom; and Life Repurposed.

At heart she is a novelist and looks forward to the day she can share her stories with the world.

Leagh blogs on hymn histories at DianaLeaghMatthews.com and plans to start a hymn-devo on social media this summer.

CONNECT WITH DIANA LEAGH MATTHEWS

WWW.DIANALEAGHMATTHEWS.COM

DiLeaghMatthews

DianaLeaghMatthews

DiLeaghMatthews

DiLeaghMattthews

DianaLeaghMatthews

Diana Leagh

NOW AVAILABLE FOR
FREE DOWNLOAD

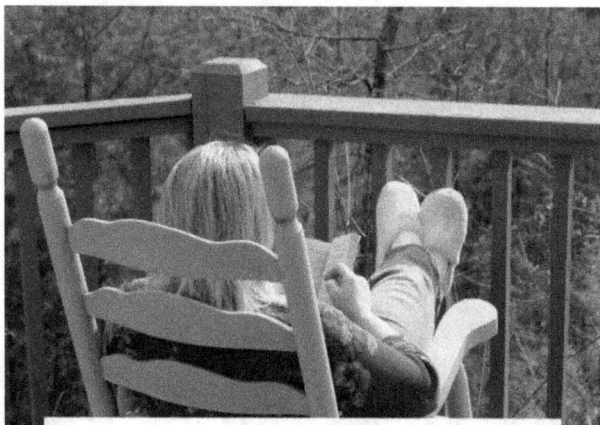

Checklist of
300+ Ways to Find
Renewal

WWW.DIANALEAGHMATTHEWS.COM
/300-WAYS-TO-FIND-RENEWAL/

NOW AVAILABLE

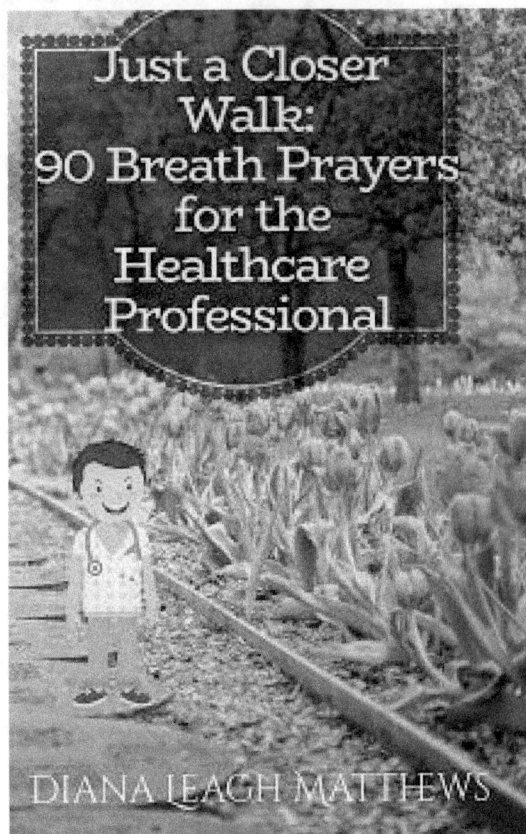

Just a Closer Walk:
90 Breath Prayers
for the
Healthcare
Professional

DIANA LEACH MATTHEWS

COMING

AUGUST 2021

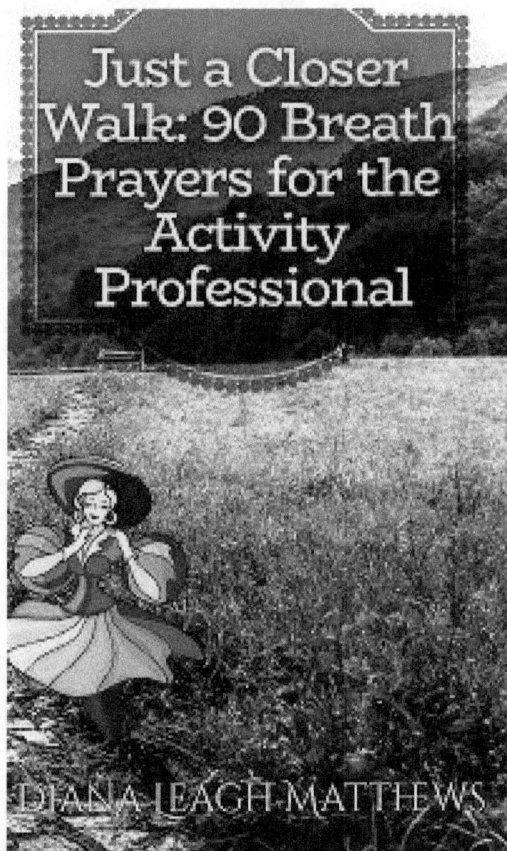

Just a Closer Walk: 90 Breath Prayers for the Activity Professional

DIANA LEAGH MATTHEWS

COMING

OCTOBER 2021

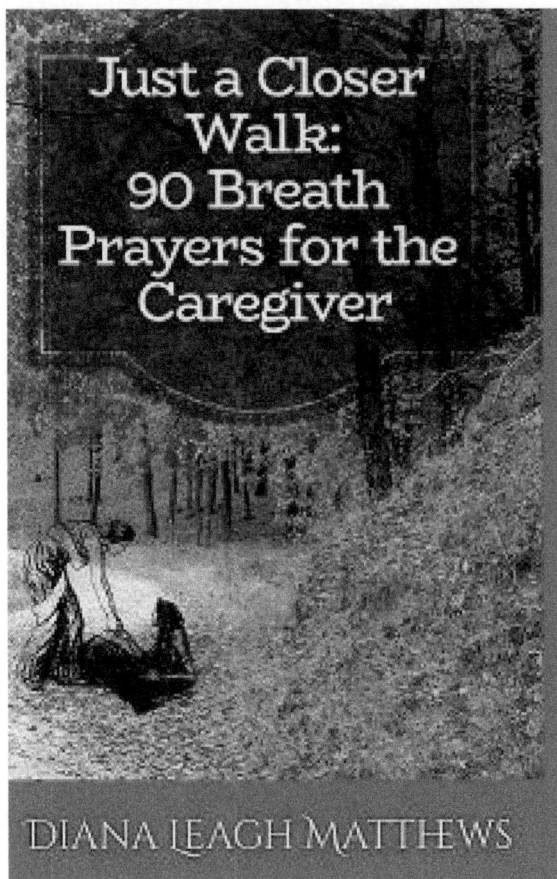

Just a Closer
Walk:
90 Breath
Prayers for the
Caregiver

DIANA LEAGH MATTHEWS

COMING

JANUARY 2022